WHAT
WILL
PEOPLE
SAY

— poems —

taniya gupta

central
avenue

2024

Published by Central Avenue Poetry, an imprint of Central Avenue Marketing Ltd.
www.centralavenuepublishing.com

WHAT WILL PEOPLE SAY

Trade Paperback: 978-1-77168-295-4
EPUB: 978-1-77168-296-1

Published in Canada
Printed in United States of America

1. POETRY / Asian American   2. POETRY / Women

1 3 5 7 9 10 8 6 4 2

Keep up with Central Avenue

for my nani
and
my mom

Dear Reader,

Thank you for being here. If you have read my work before, I want to thank you for your continued support. If this is our first encounter, welcome! I suggest you make yourself a cup of tea, and hold yourself with a lot of love as you slowly get acquainted with *What Will People Say*.

"What will people say" or *log kya kahenge* | लोग क्या कहेंगे (in Hindi) is a phrase that one hears a lot growing up in a South Asian household. From minor details like a child's clothes and meals in the lunch box, to bigger decisions like what school one should go to, what career one should pursue, and even the choice of a life partner, all are in some way dictated by the fear of society's judgment. I hope this book helps you find a path beyond the suffocating thoughts of what people might say.

Also, I am a bit of a tea nerd, and love tea as a form of self-care. I have created a tea pairing to go with each section, and if any of these teas are accessible to you, I encourage you to try them.

If you have any comments, reflections, or questions, I would absolutely love to hear from you!

With all my heart,
Taniya

trigger warnings

sexual abuse

domestic violence

attempted suicide

depression

contents

in a small town
nestled between
the lush fields of punjab
in the shadow
of the majestic himalayas
there once lived
a girl

who carried her ancestors
on her tongue
and in the color of her skin

she saw god's omens
in the mountains
and the stars

she believed
in destiny
but above all else
she believed
in herself

little girl

<u>tea pairing</u>
tea: shan lin xi
category: oolong tea
origin: taiwan
notes: a creamy oolong that often has subtle notes of
cotton candy.

did mom want me?

one early friday morning
a girl is born
her eyes still closed
her mother battling
for her own life
the doctors say
only a miracle
could keep both alive

hours of care and prayers later
she kicks her feet in excitement
as she is placed in the arms of her mother
who looks at her
with heavy-lidded eyes
smiling at the life she just created

the relatives who had gathered
waiting for the delivery
of the newborn
slowly start to disappear

the mother cradles her child
and attempts to forget about
the disappointed faces
she has seen today

does she also wish
she had given birth
to a son instead?

do not touch

the house where
my parents lived
when i was born
was a tiny rental place
in a congested neighborhood

the streets were so narrow
that cars could not get through
not that people living there
could afford a car anyways

chipped and peeling paint
decorated most walls
but the laughter of children
playing in the streets
while their mothers
exchanged the latest recipes
made it a cheerful place

my mom tells me
some of her happiest memories
from her married life
are from the four years
we spent there

when my dad had time
to play cards with her in the evenings
where the neighbors were so friendly
they would take me to their homes
for an entire day

so she could take care of the chores

charni aunty was my caretaker
whenever mom's stitches hurt
grandma refused to help
still upset at my mom
for having birthed a daughter

aunty was a tall middle-aged woman
kindness wrapped around
each wrinkle on her face
she would often take me to her neighborhood
where the houses were even smaller

she would sew clothes for my dolls
while she fed me
some achaar and roti
from her humble kitchen
i still remember
how happy and safe
i felt in her embrace

i would always insist
that she have dinner with us
she would ignore my innocent pleading
with averted eyes and a hesitant laugh
and disappear before
my dad got home

i never quite understood
this caste system

घर की लक्ष्मी | ghar ki lakshmi

when in a good mood
my dad would often exclaim
his fortune only turned
in his favor
once he married my mom

our new house was huge
large wrought iron front gate
exquisite white marble floors
tall engraved wooden doors
brass pillars along the staircase
crystal chandeliers
a never-ending affair
of glamour

most people in this
new neighborhood
had lavish mansions and fake smiles
i didn't visit the
neighbors' houses anymore
i was mostly in my room
with notebooks and pencils
writing stories
and reciting them to my dolls

mom was hurting again
not just because dad
was so busy making money
that he didn't have time
for us anymore

but also because
she was pregnant again
with only one thought occupying her mind
is it a boy this time?

a boy is born

i was five when my brother was born
my grandparents' faces lit up
when they heard the news
they decided to give
a box of desi-ghee-drenched
sweet and flaky patisa
to every family in our town
celebrating the long-awaited occasion

i was so excited to have a sibling
that i didn't question if
there had been any grand celebrations
when my parents brought me home

i was over the moon
to have a talking teddy bear
who i could call
my brother

the excitement began wearing off
when mom's attention
started going to him
instead of me

पहली लोहड़ी | pehli lohri

our house was decorated with lights
a week before lohri
halwaais were hired
invitations sent

the guests gathered around
the glowing bonfire
on that crisp winter evening

amidst the feasting, singing, and dancing
my brother was shown off
like a trophy
my family had just won

and there i stood
in a corner
observing it all
tears rolling down my cheeks

i wiped them away
with the sleeve of my blazer
my white shirt tucked into my navy-blue pants
my parents' disappointment at having a daughter
clearly evident in the clothes they dressed me in

i always say so proudly
our culture is so rich
full of festivals and colors
full of love and warmth

what i have never had the courage to say is
in our culture
a boy is a blessing from god
while a girl is considered a tragedy
you are congratulated for having a son
and consoled for
a daughter

the escape

i got off the school bus
but that day
my mom wasn't
at the door

i went into the house
searching for her

i asked my grandma
"badi-ma, mumma kahan hai?"
(grandma, where's mom?)
she looked at me
with an uneasiness on her face
and said
"aa jayegi woh"
(she will be back)

the house
usually buzzing with her voice
felt completely hollow

grandma gave me some daal and rice
but i could not swallow past the fear of asking
is she alive?

the return

hours later
i saw my grandpa and my dad
walking towards the house

i had been sitting at the doorstep
waiting for mom
my eyes still searching for her

i saw her walking behind them
eyes swollen, body trembling
clothes soaking wet

i had imagined so many stories
but not a single one
where mom was still being yelled at
as she walked through the same doors
she had used to escape that morning
to end the scoldings

i ran to her and hugged her
like i never had before
i knew i loved her
but didn't realize how much
until i lived those hours
not knowing if
i would ever hear her voice again

i whimpered
with my face drenched in tears
"mumma, fir kabhi mat jaana mujhe chor kar"
(mom, don't ever leave me again)

my motivation

my mom and i
had a very special bond
i saw her wanting to
live her dreams through me

of being an independent woman
of being a world traveler
of laughing
and being free

she would always call me
madame curie
and when i asked her why
she would say
"i don't ever want you to feel like a nobody
like your voice doesn't matter
you are an intelligent girl
who will never be dependent on a man"

home safe home

the first time i felt
a man's body on top of mine
i was barely eight

mom was blind to the fact
that there was an animal in her home
waiting to pounce
whenever she lowered her defenses

he was hired help
to clean the house
to play with us kids
and make us snacks

he became a friend
someone who had time
to take us to the park
to play games

i trusted him so much
that i only screamed
once it was too late

don't forget your place

i made up for being a daughter
by becoming an over-functioning child
i was my mom's confidante at home
and a star student at school
so even though i didn't impress them
at least my report cards did

my grades also had the benefit
of making me the teachers' favorite
and shutting up the girls in class
who teased me because
of my boyish short hair

my accomplishments
still weren't impressive enough
for one person though
*"jitna bhi padh le
coffee ke mug toh dhone hi padenge"*
*(no matter how educated you become
you'll still be the one doing the dishes)*
my grandma would always say
with a grin on her face

बेटी ही तोह है | beti hi toh hai

was my grandma's response
when asked

why my nana and nani
weren't informed
they had a granddaughter

why they weren't allowed to
visit their own daughter
who almost died
while giving birth

why mom wasn't allowed
to use the phone
to call her family

why she never
offered a smile
to mom or me

as i consoled my abused mother
i longed to be comforted myself
but all they said was
"she is so mature for her age"

— **forced to grow up too fast**

hide and seek

the joy
    of
        weightlessly
            floating
                through the air
                    on a swing
                        would make me forget about
                            many scary things

the constant fights
between my parents
the terrified face of
my little brother
our teary eyes
questioning if we could
help our mother

                    we would hold hands
                    as we went to sleep
                    telling each other
                    it would be okay next week

weeks turned into years
as we became teens
who hoped
not to be seen

                    our bodies hid
                behind the bedroom door
                while our eyes peeked
                through the keyhole

we blocked out the yelling
with pillows against our ears
and every morning got up
pretending   we couldn't hear

drama queen

the pressure i put on myself
to be the best
is probably what started
the love affair
between me
and anxiety

the first time i felt it
i said to my mother
"i think my heart wants to jump out of my chest"
she told me
"stop being dramatic, go study for your test"

we went to the doctor
to ask what was wrong
he sent me home saying
"learn to be strong"

the best girl

i was wringing my hands
sitting outside the principal's office
wondering why i had been asked
to go there immediately after
the award ceremony had concluded

i couldn't help but recount the day's events

half the school had congratulated me
since the morning
i was buzzing with excitement and nervousness
as i sat at the back of the hall

the trophy for best girl would be presented
to one girl from
the senior-most class
someone who was well rounded
participated in extracurriculars
and got good grades

i participated in most activities at school
they kept my mind off the mess
at home

ever since the sixth grade
i had imagined
what it would be like
to receive it one day

the day had finally arrived
as the principal was about to make the announcement
i imagined everyone's eyes on me
when i would be declared the winner

the award for the best girl goes to . . .
who then walked up and accepted her trophy
my senses went numb
my mind said   *run*
but my body wouldn't respond

the principal finally summoned me into her office
and after offering me a seat, explained
"you are a good student
and i have high hopes for you
but you must know that
there are certain rules
girls must follow

you refuse to tie your hair
you wear skin-tight jeans on casual days
it wouldn't set a good example
to give you the award"

holding on

i felt myself
s
i
n
k
i
n
g

many emotions clouded my thinking

was something wrong with me?

did i cause the fights between my parents?
did i tempt those men to look at me
with their hungry eyes?
did i cause my heart
to not want to stay inside my body anymore?

i didn't know the word *anxiety* back then
all i felt was my body
not wanting to be with me
like it wanted to run   away

and there was nothing
i could do
to make it
stay

bittersweet sixteen

as the black forest cake
was brought out
i noticed the
ear-to-ear smile on my grandpa's face
the chatter between my grandma and my aunts
my cousins playing and fighting at the dinner table

grandpa had reserved the country inn
the fanciest restaurant in the neighboring city
where fifteen of us went to celebrate

he would always call me *moti*
and then follow it up with
"no, you're not fat,
you are just filled with my love"

he was someone i looked up to
he lived life on his own terms
we would laugh together
fight and not talk for a few days
until one of us smiled at the other
and the argument was forgotten

i couldn't help but
feel a wave of sadness
when i noticed
someone was missing

before i even cut the cake
my uncle exclaimed

"don't be sad
that your dad is not here
he ran out of the hospital
the moment you were born
how can you expect him
to show up now?"

scrubbed clean

i was lying on
the bedroom floor
trying to make sense of it all

i didn't know that
what i really needed
was someone to tell me
"it isn't your fault"

i scanned the room
for any sharp object
i made a list of people
to say goodbye to
i reminded myself
of every reason

this world
needed to be
cleansed of me

a hopeless girl

a bottle of pills

the last phone call

standing in front of the mirror

tears streaming down

no one wants you

no one loves you

they won't care

the shame you will bring to them

i won't live for another year

clock hit 00:00

swallow

body hurts
where am i
3:55 a.m.

still here
in the living hell

should i tell them?

will they hurt me?

will they throw me out?

will they love me now?

growing up

tea pairing
tea: matcha
category: green tea
origin: japan
notes: energetic and vibrant, can be an acquired taste.

leaving the familiar

for once, i was the pride of my family
the first one to fly away
from this messy nest on a rotting tree

on a journey to fulfill
dad's desires to settle in a utopian land
and mom's hopes for me to be free

ready for my first international flight
pink cabin bag
filled half with mom's food
and half with brand-new gadgets
dad had bought for me

as i looked out the window
dreaming of the adventures ahead
a voice inside me was praying
the plane would never take off

everything i had ever known was here
the places
       the food
             the language
                  the people

my bff

to add to my
constant companions
fear, anxiety, and uncertainty

i made a new friend
as soon as i
stepped off the plane
and set foot
in canada

that friend was named
self-doubt

we had many long talks
about my choices
about being accepted
about my chances of success

whether i want it to
or not
this friend follows me around
everywhere
telling me how   i don't belong

arriving at my new home

i had imagined many times
what my first day at the university
would be like

i had pictured myself being surrounded by
grand historic buildings and
new friends

i arrived
on a brilliant september afternoon
trees exploding with color
all around the campus

exuberant volunteers
chanting the university cheers
while dancing
with black and gold pom-poms in their hands

the air was brimming with excitement
but i did not feel part of the celebrations
i was just
a spectator
observing the grand party

i walked through the cafeteria
led by a science student in his final year
smelling sweet, exotic aromas
before finally arriving at a door
with my name on it

i ran my fingers
over the hand-sketched greeting card
before entering   my new home

i shut the door and
opened my pink bag
filling the room
with the smell of mom's food

it transported me back home
into her embrace

i thought about
how far away she was
and sobbed   uncontrollably

different but all the same

i lay in my new bed
the very first night
hoping to find
some comfort and sleep

my old bed was used to me crying
this new one found it strange
trying its best to console me
it asked me not to weep

i stared at my phone
wanting to call my mom
but also trying
not to wake up my roommate

i heard the rain hitting the window
and sprung from my bed to look outside
i stared at the droplets crashing into the ground
and found solace in the familiar sound

a day on campus

waking up early morning
rushing to get ready
walking to the cafeteria
through a mob
of canada geese

sifting through breakfast options
searching for anything vegetarian
which on most days meant
a glass of cold strawberry milk and
a banana on my way to class
passing by groups of students
laughing and enjoying their freedom

my life mostly revolved around
the library and labs
there were always assignments to submit
exams to study for

i rarely ever slept before two a.m.
leaving the campus right before
the library closed for the night

i would walk back to my dorm
scared, looking around
is anyone following me?
am i safe?

i had a walking buddy
but she wasn't walking beside me

she was sitting thousands of miles away
holding the phone close to her ear
waiting for me to say *mumma, i am home*
so she could finally breathe a sigh of relief
and then do it all over again the next day

i had thought about breaking free
for so long
always pestering my parents
to send me to a boarding school

little did i know that
however complicated it was
my home was still where
my people were

i felt so lost
without them
in a country that
once was a dreamland

i shed countless tears
on my walks around campus
while eating in the cafeteria
in a corner of the library
but no one lent a shoulder

i had so many feelings to share
but i wondered
who would even care

there were plenty of people
around me
but still

  — i was alone

call 911

i call the emergency line
after missing the only bus
that would take me home
this was years before
i had internet on my phone

they told me to hang up
because the line was only
for life-threatening situations

how was this
not a life-threatening situation?

a girl was stranded
in this new land
with no one to guide her
or to hold her hand

an illicit affair

i missed my motherland
yearned for its embrace
every day

but in this new land
there was excitement
a thrill
in its unusual ways

i wanted to be loyal to who i was
but i also relished the new me

there was uncertainty with the new
but the old had inflicted many wounds

i was in trouble
i was in love with them both

was i cheating on one
when i loved the other
a little more?

becoming a woman

<u>tea pairing</u>
tea: moonlight white
category: white tea
origin: china
notes: the leaves of this tea are extremely pretty, often
resembling the moon in the night sky, and make for a
complex cup with notes of honey and wildflowers.

it doesn't   always
happen on a moonlit night sometimes it comes
at the most unexpected time   and when it does
it makes your   body tremble
the intensity   of emotions
is like nothing you have felt before
it leaves   you dancing
and speechless
— *love*

euphoria

i walked through the lavender fields
and stopped to look at a radiant flower
every part of it covered
in sparkles falling from the sky

i heard the joyful birds
and saw the dancing leaves
i felt a tingle down my spine
as the wind embraced me

a raindrop touched my forehead
and trickled down to my cheek

i held him close
as rain drenched us both
he whispered something in my ear

as our lips locked
electricity shot up from our bodies
rising up into the universe
causing lightning and thunder in the skies

after all, it was the reunion
of life and love
of earth and water

neither of us wanted to let go
it felt so right
it made us both shiver

i finally opened my eyes
with a smile on my face
i continued to dance in the rain

excerpts from my journals

1. when i am with him
   i feel cared for
   he is so amazing

2. i met his mom
   she seems sweet
   we went to watch
   zindagi na milegi dobara
   (you won't get this life again)

3. i met his dad
   he seems okay
   not the angry kind

4. i met his uncles, aunts,
   and cousins
   they were all welcoming
   but judging me with their eyes
   at the same time

   i am trying not to
   get confused

   i am trying not to
   feel overwhelmed

   i am trying not to
   screw this up

wedding planning

maybe in a year and a half

        no

                you have four months

maybe in udaipur

        no

                it will be in delhi

maybe i dance to . . .

        no

                his cousin already
                picked that song

maybe 25 guests

        no

                we already invited over 200

maybe i am suffocating

        no

                it is not as bad as mom had it

wedding crasher

taking the first step towards my new life
i walked under a chaadar of roses
that was held up by my brother and cousins

diamonds and gold adorned my neck
an intricately embroidered mint blue dupatta
framed my face
complementing my pink lehenga

my hands and feet covered in dark brown mehndi
the strength of its color, i was told, predicted
the love and affection i would receive
from my mother-in-law

the chuda that i had been so excited to wear
dazzled from the lights shining on me
the pearl-covered kaleere hanging from my wrists
chimed as i took each step

filled with excitement
that transformed into nervousness
as i looked up and saw
a crowd of unfamiliar faces

looking at me
with amazement or horror
i will never know

i had heard of strangers crashing weddings
but i could never have imagined
a bride feeling like one at her own

the calm inside the storm

as i waded through the sea
of phones and cameras
tracking my every movement
a million thoughts
went through my head

who are these people?
do i look okay?
am i doing this right?
do i want to do this?

i saw his face
the guy who taught me
the meaning of love
who stood by my side
through thick and thin
waiting there for me patiently

i finally took a deep breath
my steps lengthened in stride
moving closer and closer to him
as my heart reminded me how much
he loves me

बंधन | bandhan

she is not just someone's wife
but also someone's new sister-in-law
someone's new daughter (in-law)

many new relationships
in a blink of an eye

can she cook?
can she clean?
will she give us grandchildren?

does she? can she? will she?

i feel the weight
it withers me down
i ask myself

how will i ever live up to everything
that is now expected of me?

संस्कारी बहू | sanskari bahu

we are taught from an early age
a sanskari bahu does not talk back
to her husband or her in-laws

my cousin kept quiet when
her husband hit her
because he was drunk
she concealed her bruises
saying she had tripped
if we ever caught a glimpse

my aunt complied every afternoon when
my uncle kicked her out of their room
so he could fuck the maid
she held back her tears every time we asked
why she was sitting in the verandah under the hot sun

another aunt obeyed when
my uncle ordered her to stand naked outside their bedroom
as a punishment for offending him
she hid her shame in the dark
as she prayed for mother earth to engulf her

my mom didn't fight back when
my dad slapped her
because her cooking wasn't good enough
she tried to convince us every morning
that our dad was a good man

i had seen too many failed marriages

and should have known better
but like they say
love is blind

if it's not the husband
then it's the in-laws
telling you that your   feelings
have no space in the
box they created for you

i see the fear in my mom's eyes
when i tell her about the things
being said to me by my other family

i hear the pain in her voice
as she tells me to be strong
and that it will all be okay

but how, mom?
how will i ever be good enough for them?

i start chanting *"ram ram"*
and i feel a sense of peace

i don't know if it's the words
that calm me down
or the memories of my mother
chanting the same mantra

it happened every time
someone yelled at her
or threw food back at her face
because it wasn't hot enough

how many more generations
will it take before this society
stops burying girls
under the weight
of countless expectations?

— ***ram ram***

it's another night

years and years later
and i am that little girl again
curled up in her bed
terrified listening for any movement
any sound in the house

my thoughts and my heart rate
seem to be competing
should parents send an instruction manual
when they send their daughter off
to her new house?

are these in-laws not taught
how to treat a girl?

it's another night
years and years later
and i am that little girl again
curled up in her bed
petrified because the moment i tried
to contradict my mother-in-law
she yelled at me so loud
that the sound still echoes in my head

mom wouldn't let me get off the bed
on the days i was sick
or had blood dripping down my legs
but this lady hands me a mop anyways

sometimes i wonder

if this is all worth it
or if it's better
to just run away

it's another night
years and years later
but nothing has changed

crashing down

tea pairing
tea: tulsi
category: herbal tea
origin: india
notes: tulsi is a type of basil considered holy in india. i find
tulsi tea to be very supportive for my mental health. it also
reminds me of my nani praying to her tulsi plant every
morning for its healing powers.

i   feel   tied   down
by   unbreakable   chains   i   try
to pull myself out   i try to   quiet the noise
i sit to meditate my mind slows down
i see myself at a beach i feel the waves
touching my feet i see mountains in the distance

breathe   in   breathe   out

as soon as i open my eyes i realize
the chains followed me to the shore
i had plans i have plans
is there a point in
living with restraints?
"there is hope" they say
i watch it fading
a w a y

the internal battle

my mind, my thoughts
how real are they?
are they even mine?

yes
they are saying bad things about you.

no
they are not
how can they
they barely know me

no
your dad doesn't care about you

yes
he totally does
how can he not
hasn't he been there for me all these years

i want to believe what my mind tells me
i want to just agree and stop the battle
but deep down there is a part of me
that doesn't see eye to eye with it

my body is tired of it all
it doesn't know how to end this war
but day after day
it still takes me to places near and far

i wish there was a switch i could flip
to turn this mind off
to shut these eyes closed
to fill this heart with love
and just open the door
to let life in

growing up   i saw all disagreements   answered with anger   i learnt to meet my problems with fury   that gave people the opportunity   to call me a monster   they started provoking me   trying to get a reaction out of me   only to then say   *you are out of control*   once i left home   i quickly realized anger was not how most people solved their problems   showing my wrath   only drove people away   i started to suppress the rage within   it would shake my whole body at times   the tremors from the earthquake   would release tsunamis from my eyes   deep chasms forming in my mind   but i refused to let anyone else be destroyed   by the monster within

my conditioning

when
you made me cry
i blamed me

when
your mother called me fat
i blamed me

when
your father said i would destroy your life
i blamed me

when
your sister-in-law called me immature
i blamed me

when
your uncle called me too picky
i blamed me

when
your aunt called me chalaak
i blamed me

i always blamed me
for not knowing how to be

hanging by a thread

trust breaks
when parents don't show up
to rescue their children in danger

when you speak your heart out to a friend
and they spill your secrets

when you let someone get close enough to see your tears
and they tell you to not be a child

and once it breaks
no apology, promise, or reassurance
can heal the scars left behind

trust is a mala
108 beads held together by a thread
but once broken
can never be put together
the same way again

cover up

i was walking home / a little girl / a boy ran my way / squeezed my
breast / he laughed / i cried / on a plane by myself / sitting next to
a white british man / lights went dim / his hand went up my top /
i froze / until i didn't / a final interview / a dream life in new york
/ his eyes fixated on my cleavage / of all the questions i should have
asked / did i wear the wrong top / another interview years later /
impressive resume / is that an engagement ring / where do you live /
i can drop you home every night / why i hide my body

hell

i was being attacked
from left, right, and center
by my fears, my anxieties,
my negative thoughts

i felt
like i
couldn't
breathe

even though i had just woken up
i yearned for night again
because then
i could just lie down in bed
and not have to move

no matter how hard i tried
everything was coming
crashing down

so this is what hell feels like

it's not in some
unknown part of this universe
it's right up here
in our heads

maybe my internal scale is broken

i either love too much   or   not at all

i want to talk to you all the time   or   not hear from you ever again

i will drench you to the bone   and   not have a drop to offer
some days   your parched throat on others

there is never   an   in-between

— imbalanced

when i wake up feeling anxious

i ask myself
what is it that you are longing for?
for all that's there is within you
then why do you feel incomplete?

i ask the universe
to send me the answers
in the warmth of the sun
and in the cool of the wind

but
i hear   nothing

i see the lavender flowers
dancing in the breeze
i smell their soothing fragrance
and it makes my heart rejoice
i feel the angels dance around me
and the light inside me starts to shine

i long for a world
full of compassion
where we nurture one another
where we see the depth in our souls
and the hunger in our hearts

where we unite in love
and not divide in hate
where we accept the differences
and not alienate

a ray of hope

when someone shows me affection
i cling onto them
i give them my whole heart
that has been longing for some comfort

can you blame me
for trying time and again
to climb out of
this dark well

after the first heartbreak / i laid down a few bricks /
and then a few more /   used the tears as a cement to
bind them /   the fire inside
helped forge   the metal spikes
for the top /   when the time came
to tear it down /   i realized how rigid
it had gotten   over the years / now
i am in this fortress i carefully built / it's dark and lonely /
            and i can't find a way out

पर सहम जाता हूं मैं, माँ | par saham jata hoon main, ma

whenever my brother was
yelled at or spanked
he would never fight back

once my parents' rage subsided
they would say
"*saham jata hai ye*"

saham (सहम) is a term in hindi
used to describe
someone gone quiet
usually a child who doesn't say a lot
and looks afraid

is *saham* a child's way of saying
i have gone through trauma—
physical, mental, emotional
there is too much noise
in my head
i can't process this hate
i need love
i have so much to say
but i can't find the right words
help me . . . ?

all the times
i told you
i don't need you

what i really meant was
i can take care of myself

i have been doing it
since i was very little
but now that i know
what love really feels like

i just want you
to hold me
will you?

your family wants me
to fit into a mold that
i wasn't made for

i will suffocate
i don't want to

save me,
will you?

   — a letter to my husband

the search is on

i repeatedly check the doors and windows
and look behind the shower curtain
searching for intruders

they tell me i am paranoid
have they been robbed of safety
in their own home?

left so broken
that it took years to collect
the shattered pieces

my healing

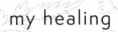

<u>tea pairing</u>
tea: ginger masala chai
category: black tea
origin: india
notes: a warming and comforting mix of ginger, spices, and
black tea. my own healing journey has involved many cups
of ginger masala chai.

दहलीज़ | dehlīz

i am standing at the door
behind me is the pain, the shattered dreams, the shame
gripping onto my legs
begging me not to go through

telling me life isn't easy on the other side
anxiety has me by the neck in the moment
there is so much that is unknown

and yet, there is a part of me that
wants to open the door
let the new possibilities
take my hand and pull me in

emdr

as i sat there in the therapist's office
she asked me to follow her finger
as she moved it left and right

for the first few moments
i thought it was silly
until a flood of memories
came rushing at me

there i was
a little girl
with a head full of dreams
standing proudly on the stage
accepting my award
eyes fixated on the audience
scanning each row for my dad
he promised he would show up this time

there i was again
confused why this strange man
was putting mustard oil between my legs
he made me swear
never to say a word about it to anyone

through my sessions in my therapist's office
i met so many versions of me
that had been betrayed

years had passed
i had never even let myself cry

over some of the heartaches
but once the gates opened
there was no way to save the dam
i had so carefully built

at the end of each session
the therapist reminded me
"forgive them,
learn to be your own parent"

these words that initially irked me
slowly started to sink in
as i picked up all the broken pieces
reminding myself with each breath

i am a survivor
i will be okay

cutting loose

i am a kite
meant to soar high
but the string to my dreams
got tangled with the expectations
of the ones it was handed to

the light within

i opened all the doors and windows
i lit a candle in each room

everything that was hiding in the dark
the traumas, the fears
all started crawling out

i sat down with each one
i listened to their stories
i let myself cry

when the sun came out
and its rays pierced through
they all started to slither away

one by one
i let them all go
said goodbye to the unwelcome guests

i redecorated each room with memories
of me and mom
of conversations with my brother
of plans made with dad to change the world
of adventures with my husband

i reminded myself
of everything
i had survived

and all that lay
ahead of me

universe to the rescue

earth said, i'll hold you child
the fire underneath her skin
started to rise

she felt the water
hold her gently
making her dance
in her own skin

sweat trickled down
as the flame engulfed
everything she didn't need anymore

she felt so light
yet so connected with the universe
as it all came together

she couldn't contain her joy
or her energy
she knew a storm was brewing

the wind caressed her skin
as she whispered to herself
let me feel everything
that i have been scared to feel,
because today
the universe holds me safe within itself

संकल्प | sankalpa

yes i made mistakes
did terrible things too
i have been running away
from the shame and guilt

but does the sun stop shining
because its heat caused wildfires somewhere
or does the river stop flowing
because floods destroyed someone's home?

then how can i?

i am planting
seeds of change
nurturing them
with faith and resilience

and watching
the new me
emerge

changing with the seasons

as i sit down
with my cup of tea
i look at the trees
changing colors
and shedding their leaves

i feel the warmth of my mug
against my own shedding skin

i remind myself
it's okay to change
it's okay to be selfish
it's okay
to just be you

when i realized i had
let others craft
the book of my life

defining my role in every chapter
writing my character
as the villain
time and again

the antagonist who
didn't do as told
who questioned too
many age-old traditions

i took it in my hands
and ripped out the pages
that didn't belong
i pulled them so hard
my fingers bled

despite the pain
i smiled

i now had space
to write

— my story

i got the moves

some days   when everyone in my house was busy
i would just put on music   and dance for hours   it
didn't matter   if i was good or not   it made me smile
made me forget about   all the hurt   and fear
inside me   so to the "friends"   who have laughed at me
(i saw you)   take your   perfect dance moves
somewhere else   because in my world   we dance
because   it makes us happy   we put on a show
just for ourselves   and we will continue dancing
no matter   how much this world tells us
how imperfect we are

innate

even though
english is what my tongue
is comfortable with now
to this day
when expressing my purest emotions
my heart and mind talk to me in hindi

except
when my temper flares
and i feel the urge to
go on the offense

then
i can only find the words
in english

this puzzled me
until
i recognized

anger is not something
i was born with
it's something the world
forced me to learn
as it took
my innocence away

sorry, not sorry

i have countless notes on my phone
attempts to gather my thoughts
to prepare for conversations

apologizing to my new "parents"
for things i did that upset them
for things my parents didn't do
for things my sister-in-law doesn't do
that i have to compensate for
for things i don't want to do
but they try to persuade me
saying "*log kya kahenge?*" *(what will people say?)*

i am getting tired
because
even after all the effort
i get nothing in return

to tell you the truth
i am not sorry
for the   space   i take
for standing up for myself
for not wanting to follow traditions blindly
for not talking to people who insult me
or for marrying your son

i am not sorry
that i exist

focus

i love you
but your existence
in my life
is toxic
to my own

i know you said i was
"me focused" and
even though
you meant that as
a negative trait

i took it
as a compliment

i am focused on me
on prioritizing my well-being
over pleasing you

secure your own mask first

self-love doesn't come easy to us women
we are taught that if we don't live our lives
serving and prioritizing others
we are not good daughters
good sisters
good wives
good daughters-in-law
or good mothers

we are being selfish

we are born with the desire
to nurture everything
but somehow we forget that
we wildflowers need rain too

so my dear, buy yourself some flowers
bake yourself a cake
open that expensive bottle of wine
who said candlelight dinners
have to be for two?

we are all afraid of dying

the other day someone asked me
"what is your biggest fear in life?"

i am wondering
what a person like me
can be afraid of
after coming so close
to taking my own life
not once but twice

staring in the mirror
and not recognizing
the person standing
on the other side

looking down from the terrace
above a twelfth-floor apartment
not knowing what to do with
this ghost of a girl
living inside my body

so to answer the question,
"my biggest fear
is losing myself
again"

going from your worst to your best

it's one baby step at a time / it's getting out of bed before 9 a.m. /
it's pushing open the curtains when you have been engulfed by the
darkness in your head for far too long / it's finding your walking shoes
and clearing the dust off them / it's looking in the mirror and telling
yourself things that you might not believe in that very moment / you
can do it / just ten minutes / maybe fifteen tomorrow / it's learning
to close your eyes again when you hear the birdsong / it's embracing
the warmth of the sun on your skin / it's admiring the hibiscus flowers
that line the path / it's slowly gaining trust in your own self / to wake
up / to walk / to just breathe . . .

lioness

don't mistake my softness for my weakness
don't treat my tears as my breaking point
don't take my vulnerability as an open invitation

let me remind you that
a mother has the softest heart
until she senses danger around her child
and then you see her transform into a lioness
her roars shake the jungle
sending every predator
running back to their den

and let me tell you
a woman can be her own mother
when she needs to be

so back off rapist
i am not a little girl anymore
new parents
i trusted you with my tears one too many times
evil world
i am coming for you

reunite, rejoice

tea pairing
tea: darjeeling
category: black tea
origin: india
notes: a celebration calls for a cup of darjeeling tea. an
aromatic and refreshing black tea, also known as the
champagne of tea.

you ~~were~~ are a free bird

छोड़ आए हम वो गलियाँ | chhod aaye hum woh galiyan

(*we have left those streets behind*)
but my heart seems to be in denial
my eyes still look for my brother
my mouth still waters at the thought
of mom's aloo paranthe
my ears still long for dad's voice
my nose awaits the smell
of the guava tree in our backyard

musafir hoon yaaron
(*i am a traveler, o friends*)
but i still miss my home
this journey of life
has taken me to many places
but the music in my words
is an ode to where it all began
the color of my skin
paints a picture
of the land
i come from

homesick

immersed now in the new ways
i love exploring this adventure-filled land
friends have become my family
and visits back home are scant

but still, in times of extreme joy
and immense sadness,
i find myself turning to
pleasures left behind

i look for that old blanket
and wrap my inner child in it
i listen to music almost forgotten,
the tunes that had been my companions once

they bring me back to my safe place
and fill my heart with a soothing warmth
like the first sip of chai on a bitter morning
reviving me from my muddled haze

my roots

i started running
away from my roots
i feared they made me

                        stand out

i held back
my tongue
i wanted to belong
guided
by my self-doubt

it took me too long
to realize
that my roots
were my strength
they stayed with me
no matter
how far i went

not stand out
they helped me stand

they nourished me
and made me
who i am

ruk jana nahin tu kahin haar ke
they tell us to keep going
get rich or die trying
because that's what will keep
the economy growing

kanton pe chal ke milenge saaye bahaar ke
suffer now to reap the rewards later
when has trading our
mind, body, and family
for a bigger bank balance
brought about
a happily-ever-after?

yun hi chala chal rahi
but these days won't come back
slow down
hold your daughter in your arms
while you still can because
tomorrow
she won't be so little anymore
tomorrow
she might forget how to smile and
tomorrow
you might wonder
when you heard
her laughter last

— dedicated to my papa

tips for dealing with uncertainty

make yourself a warm cup of tea
light an incense or a candle
settle in with a fuzzy blanket by a window

now as the tea and incense fill your senses
look at the vast sky above you and
the birds flying freely
remind yourself that
nothing about their day is certain

the trees outside don't know if
they will get rain, breeze, or sunshine
they continue to
stand tall and provide us shade

you, my dear, are a part of this universe
that cracks, explodes, and yet
continues to move

so will you

not a mirror

on my first day at the university
i met this girl
who looked nothing like me
or the people i had been around
all my life
and yet i felt like saying hello

we have stood by each other
through all-nighters
lent a shoulder to the other
through heartaches and
traveled across continents together

i now proudly call her
my bestie

how is it that even after
all the lines they drew and
the walls they built
i still find them

my people
who love living each moment
whose resilience inspires others
who believe in
community over competition

in creating a tribe
however big or small
to hold space when needed

my people
don't have to be like me
they just have to understand
my values
and
i theirs

finding home

the first time you opened your eyes / the first time you learnt lohri celebrations are only for sons / the first time you felt a grown man's weight on top of you / the first time you saw mom bang her head against a wall over and over / the first time you kissed your childhood sweetheart / the first time you decided to cleanse the world of yourself / the first time someone chased you to your house / the first time you got on a plane all by yourself / the first time you saw pride in papa's eyes / the first time you moved to another country / the first time you jumped out of a plane and screamed "i am free" / the first time you hiked a volcano and thought you were almost going to die / wasn't i right there with you, baby girl? / so go on / live your life / love your life / because no matter how many times you fall / you break / you cry / i will take you / i will love you over and over again / i will be here

this world is full of girls
girls with dreams
girls with questions

why (not) her?

why can her brother go out
alone at night
but not her?

why wasn't she invited
to that office party?

girls dealing with
society telling them
they should just stay home
and raise kids

what we need is to empower,
educate, and enable each other
to go after our dreams,
and remind one another

— you matter

our fight

i had to fight
for my existence
before i was even
out of my mother's womb

i didn't stop
fighting then
why would i
stop now?

reunite

somewhere on this journey
under the weight of the obligations
and all the expectations
i lost touch with that little girl

the one who used to
follow her heart
without inhibition

the one who didn't filter
every decision with
what will people say?

why am i so afraid now?

i want to bring that little girl
on this journey with me
let her teach me
how to break the shackles

i want to dance with her
throw the weight off my shoulders
rejoice in
being unbound

a mantra for the reader as you go on in your journey:

breathe

and

trust that

you're enough

Glossary

achaar, from the poem "do not touch," p. 4-5.
Pickled food, usually made from a variety of fruits and vegetables.

aloo paranthe, from the poem "छोड़ आए हम वो गलियाँ | chhod aaye hum woh galiyan," p. 98.
Plural form of aloo parantha, a type of flatbread made with potato and flour, fried in a pan. It is a comfort food often enjoyed by Punjabi families on the weekend.

bandhan, from the poem "बंधन | bandhan," p. 50.
Ties or bonds, usually between people

beti hi toh hai, from the poem "बेटी ही तोह है | beti hi toh hai," p. 16.
Literal translation: "it's just a daughter," a phrase often used to diminish the value of a daughter.

chaadar, from the poem "wedding crasher," p. 48.
A sheet or a covering. In certain South Asian cultures, when a bride walks to the altar, she is escorted by her brothers and/or male cousins, who hold an adorned sheet (sometimes crafted of flowers) above her, which symbolizes the love and care she has been raised with.

chalaak, from the poem "my conditioning," p. 63.
Cunning

chhod aaye hum woh galiyan, from the poem "छोड़ आए हम वो गलियाँ | chhod aaye hum woh galiyan," p. 98.
The title and lyric of a Hindi song, where the literal translation is "we have left those streets behind."

chuda, from the poem "wedding crasher," p. 48.
A set of red bangles traditionally worn in Punjabi weddings by a bride, gifted by her mother's side of the family. They are often worn for the first full year of the marriage, signifying that the woman wearing them is a new bride.

daal, from the poem "the escape," p. 11.
Lentils

dehlīz, from the poem "दहलीज़ | dehlīz," p. 77.
A Hindi word with origin in Farsi. It roughly translates to the floor in a doorway, or the entrance, or the boundary before we cross to the other side.

desi-ghee, from the poem "a boy is born," p. 8.
Clarified butter, commonly used in Indian cooking.

dupatta, from the poem "wedding crasher," p. 48.
A piece of fabric, similar to a shawl, worn with traditional outfits in some South Asian cultures. A bridal dupatta is usually hand embroidered with gold threadwork, and is often the centerpiece of the bride's wedding outfit.

kaleere, from the poem "wedding crasher," p. 48.
Gold or silver embellished ornamental hangings worn by a Punjabi bride on her wedding day, attached to her chuda (see above) or bangles.

kanton pe chal ke milenge saaye bahaar ke, from "dedicated to my papa," p. 101.
The title and lyric of a Hindi song, where the literal translation of the phrase is "by walking on thorns you will get the shade of spring."

lakshmi, from the poem "घर की लक्ष्मी | ghar ki lakshmi," p. 6.
The Hindu goddess of wealth and prosperity. This poem explores the irony of daughters and daughters-in-law being referred to as Lakshmi of the house while being abused.

lohri, from the poem "पहली लोहड़ी | pehli lohri," p. 9.
A festival that is celebrated in the winter month of January in northern India. This poem explores the tradition of celebrating the first lohri for newborn sons.

lehenga, from the poem "wedding crasher," p. 48.
A full-length skirt, usually of a luxurious fabric and glamorous design, worn by South Asian women on special occasions.

halwaai, from the poem "पहली लोहड़ी | pehli lohri," p. 9.
Plural form of halwaai, a traditional Indian dessert chef hired for special occasions and set up in the backyard of a house to make food and sweets for guests.

mala, from the poem "hanging by a thread," p. 64.
A Sanskrit term for a string of beads, usually used for spiritual chanting, and typically containing 108 beads.

mehndi, from the poem "wedding crasher," p. 48.
Henna—many South Asian cultures practice women (especially brides) getting elaborate henna art drawn on their hands, arms, and feet for festivals and weddings.

musafir hoon yaaron, from the poem "छोड़ आए हम वो गलियाँ | chhod aaye hum woh galiyan," p. 98.
The title and lyric of a Hindi song, where the literal translation is "I am a traveler, o friends."

nana, from the poem "बेटी ही तोह है | beti hi toh hai," p. 16.
Maternal grandfather

nani, from the poem "बेटी ही तोह है | beti hi toh hai," p. 16.
Maternal grandmother

par saham jata hoon main, ma, from the poem "पर सहम जाता हूं मैं, माँ | par saham jata hoon main, ma," p. 71.
The lyrics of a Hindi song called "Meri Maa" (my mother), roughly translates to "But I get scared, Mom." This song talks about a kid in distress, crying to his mother for help.

patisa, from the poem "a boy is born," p. 8.
An Indian dessert made with sugar, flour, and desi-ghee.

ram ram, from the poem "ram ram," p. 53.
Lord Ram is a Hindu god, and Ram Ram is a mantra people often chant during prayers or meditation. The mantra is believed to give the devotee willpower and enhance their mental energy.

roti, from the poem "do not touch," p. 4-5.
A type of flatbread usually made with whole wheat flour.

ruk jana nahin tu kahin haar ke, from the poem "dedicated to my papa," p. 101.
The title and lyric of a Hindi song, where the literal translation of the phrase is "Don't you give up and stop."

saham, from the poem "पर सहम जाता हूं मैं, माँ | par saham jata hoon main, ma," p. 71.
A Hindi term used to describe a mix of fear and timidity.

sankalpa, from the poem "संकल्प | sankalpa," p. 83.
A Sanskrit word for an intention or a deep commitment formed by the heart and mind.

sanskari bahu, from the poem "संस्कारी बहू | sanskari bahu," p. 51.
Translates to "a cultured daughter-in-law." The phrase refers to the expectations in South Asian cultures of how a daughter-in-law or wife should always put her husband's and in-laws' needs before her own, and be on her best behavior in society in order to bring pride to her new family.

yun hi chala chal rahi, from the poem "dedicated to my papa," p. 101.
The title and lyric of a Hindi song, where the literal translation of the phrase is "Keep on walking, o traveler."

zindagi na milegi dobara, from the poem "excerpts from my journals," p. 46.
A Bollywood movie, the literal translation of the title being "You won't get this life again" or a way of saying "you only live once."

Notes

a hopeless girl (p. 27) is inspired by Elizabeth Acevedo's *Clap When You Land*

an illicit affair (p. 40) was originally published in *Brown Girl Magazine*

sanskari bahu (p. 51) was originally published in *Brown Girl Magazine*

not a mirror (p. 103) is inspired by the work of Fatimah Asghar and Safia Elhillo

finding home (p. 105) is inspired by Ellen Bass's poem "The Thing Is"

देवनगरी | Devanagari

The text that appears in Hindi in this book is using Devanagari script, which is an ancient script used to write many languages including Sanskrit, Hindi, and Nepali. The script is phonetic, so each letter is pronounced as it is written. I learnt to write English before I learnt any other language, but I grew up listening to and speaking many beautiful languages—Hindi, Punjabi, and Urdu. Even though this book is primarily written in English, I wanted to include some bits of Hindi to acknowledge and honor my fascination with the richness of language.

Incredibly grateful for . . .

my brother, thank you for sharing this life, these experiences and memories with me. You are the best gift our parents ever gave me.

my husband, thank you for always making me feel like I belong, and for being a huge part of this book journey.

my mom, thank you for instilling faith and love in me. You are my biggest rockstar!

my dad, for dreaming a dream and forcing me to be independent.

my friend Kartik, thank you for always being there no matter what, no matter when.

my friend Diana—thank you for being the one place I never have to perform, I can just exist and breathe.

Alicia, the first time I met you in person, I felt like I could dream bigger dreams. Thank you for everything!

Jasmin, thank you for helping me find my poet voice.

Rupi, thank you for telling the world that brown girl voices matter.

Ari, thank you for giving me courage to write about some very difficult times.

my friend Chintu, you sparked the dream in me that I could write a book.

my sister Esha, thank you for reading so many first drafts of my work, and always encouraging me to write.

my mentor/friend/guide Veena, I wouldn't be where I am without your love, encouragement, and support. You're my angel.

my teacher Sooz, thank you for being a part of my healing journey, for teaching me softness and the art of slowing down. I am incredibly grateful for your presence and guidance in my life.

Jahnavi Harrison, whose music helped me float my boat towards healing so I could write the second half of this book.

my teachers Adam and Sandra—thank you for being there and helping me find my path.

my friends Jann, Traci, Lu Ann, Nazanin, Soo, Sara, Mona, Cody (and others who I might have missed to mention here), you have brought joy and trust back into my life. My life is so enriched with all of you in it . . . Thank you. :)

my friends/guides/mentors—Gayatri aunty and Neha P—thank you for believing in me, and always sending me pyaar and honsla.

the team at Central Avenue—Michelle, Beau, Jess, Molly—thank you for believing in me, for your guidance, and for helping me bring my work to the world . . . I am extremely grateful for you every day.

Fatima—thank you for designing the cover of my dreams.

my readers—THANK YOU from the bottom of my heart for just being you!

About the Author

Taniya Gupta is a poet who grew up in Punjab, India, and now lives in the suburbs of Toronto, Canada. Her love for poetry started at a very young age, when writing her thoughts down on paper was the only way she knew how to process her emotions. Now, she writes as a means of healing and connecting with others who may otherwise feel they are alone in their struggles.

What Will People Say is her debut collection of poems, inspired by not only her own life, but also the women in her family and millions of others trapped in patriarchal family structures. Taniya's hope is to offer her readers a sense of connection and a guilt-free path towards their own healing.

Outside of poetry, Taniya loves looking for moments of slowness through yoga and tea.

Instagram @yogateapoetry

TikTok @taniya_yogateapoetry

yogateapoetry.com

this is for all the women
who love to dream
and are ready to carve
their own path